Big Trucks

FIRST EDITION

DK LONDON: Series Editor Deborah Lock; **Art Director** Martin Wilson;
Pre-Production Producer Nadine King; **Producer** Sara Hu; **Jacket Designer** Martin Wilson;
Reading Consultant Linda Gambrell, PhD; **DK DELHI: Senior Editor** Priyanka Nath;
Senior Art Editor Rajnish Kashyap; **Assistant Editor** Deeksha Saikia; **Assistant Designer** Tanvi Sahu;
DTP Designer Anita Yadav; **Picture Researcher** Sumedha Chopra

THIS EDITION
Editorial Management by Oriel Square
Produced for DK by WonderLab Group LLC
Jennifer Emmett, Erica Green, Kate Hale, *Founders*

Editors Grace Hill Smith, Libby Romero, Michaela Weglinski;
Photography Editors Kelley Miller, Annette Kiesow, Nicole DiMella;
Managing Editor Rachel Houghton; **Designers** Project Design Company; **Researcher** Michelle Harris;
Copy Editor Lori Merritt; **Indexer** Connie Binder; **Proofreader** Larry Shea;
Reading Specialist Dr. Jennifer Albro; **Curriculum Specialist** Elaine Larson

Published in the United States by DK Publishing
1745 Broadway, 20th Floor, New York, NY 10019
Copyright © 2023 Dorling Kindersley Limited
DK, a Division of Penguin Random House LLC
22 23 24 25 26 10 9 8 7 6 5 4 3 2 1
001-333885-May/2023

A catalog record for this book
is available from the Library of Congress.
HC ISBN: 978-0-7440-7161-0
PB ISBN: 978-0-7440-7162-7

DK books are available at special discounts when purchased in bulk for sales promotions, premiums,
fundraising, or educational use. For details, contact: DK Publishing Special Markets,
1745 Broadway, 20th Floor, New York, NY 10019
SpecialSales@dk.com

Printed and bound in China

The publisher would like to thank the following for their kind permission to reproduce their images:
a=above; c=center; b=below; l=left; r=right; t=top; b/g=background
Dreamstime.com: Alterfalter 3c
Cover images: *Front:* **Shutterstock.com:** Mechanik, MotionSky Studio ca;
Back: **Shutterstock.com:** Evgen_diz_art cra, ViGor Art cla

All other images © Dorling Kindersley
For more information see: www.dkimages.com

For the curious
www.dk.com

Big Trucks

Contents

Trucks

Trucks are BIG.
Trucks are heavy.

Trucks pull and
carry loads.

Flatbed Trucks

The flatbed truck carries loads on its trailer.

trailer

load

Tow Trucks

The tow truck carries a broken-down car.

arm —

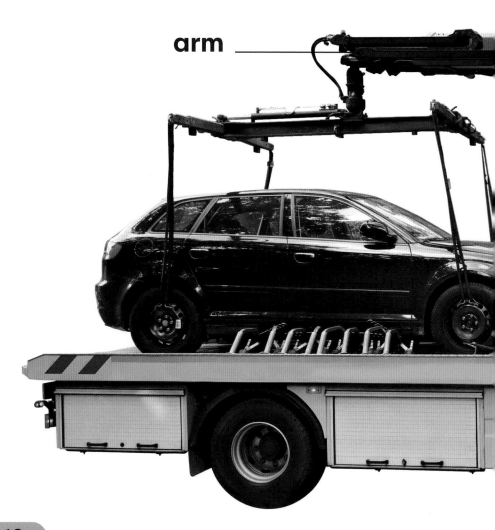

tow hitch

**exhaust
pipe**

Big Rigs

The big rig pulls many trailers on long trips.

trailer

Road Rollers

The heavy road roller flattens the road.

drum roller

Forklift Trucks

The forklift truck lifts and moves heavy loads.

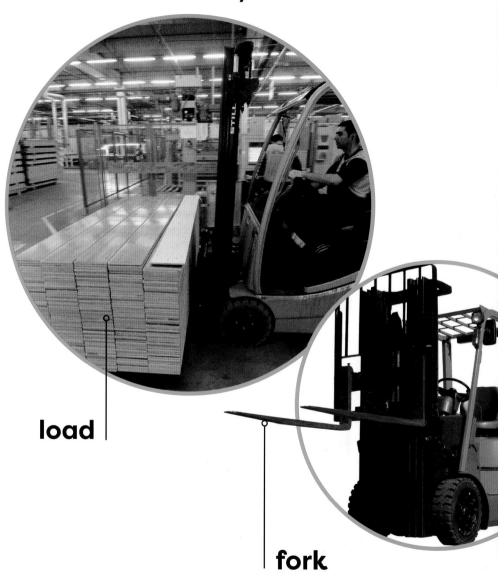

load

fork

driver

Wheel Loaders

The wheel loader scoops up large rocks.

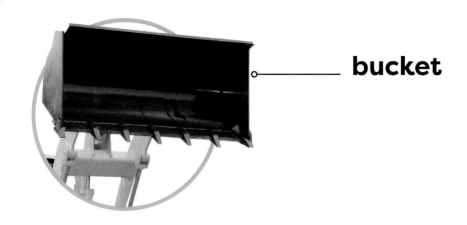

bucket

rock

Dump Trucks

The dump truck tips up its back so the rubble slides out.

open-box bed

cab

Excavators

The excavator digs trenches with its shovel.

track

shovel

Compactors

The compactor presses down on garbage with its spiked wheels.

spiked wheel

Fire Trucks

The fire trucks have hoses and ladders to help put out fires.

ladder _____○

hose

Monster Trucks

The monster truck does stunts on its huge wheels.

hood

wheel

Glossary

compactor
a machine that squashes waste or soil into smaller spaces

excavator
a machine that has a cab and bucket on a turning platform

forklift truck
a truck that lifts and moves loads

monster truck
a pickup truck with very large wheels for doing stunts

wheel loader
a machine with a bucket to dig out earth and rocks

Index

Quiz

Answer the questions to see what you have learned. Check your answers with an adult.

1. What does a tow truck carry?

2. What does an excavator do?

3. What kind of truck can lift and move heavy loads?

4. What do fire trucks use to help put out fires?

5. Talk about your favorite kind of truck. What does it do or carry?

1. A broken-down car 2. It digs trenches with its shovel
3. A forklift truck 4. Hoses and ladders 5. Answers will vary